Original title:
Arbor's Aria

Copyright © 2025 Creative Arts Management OÜ
All rights reserved.

Author: Dante Kingsley
ISBN HARDBACK: 978-1-80567-024-7
ISBN PAPERBACK: 978-1-80567-104-6

A Chime in the Shade

Beneath the boughs a squirrel prances,
With acorns stored in funny glances.
The tree's old branch creaks with a laugh,
As birds attempt a wobbly craft.

A breeze ticks leaves, a playful tease,
But watch your hat—it's caught with ease!
The sun peeks in with a wink so bright,
While shadows dance in pure delight.

The Forest's Whispering Song

The trees debate in rustling tones,
About the weather and the stones.
A bear hums low, a funny beat,
As rabbits jiggle on their feet.

The mushrooms giggle, sprouting wide,
While crickets chirp—oh, what a ride!
The wind joins in, a merry cheer,
As nature's band plays loud and clear.

Poetic Ponderings of the Pines

Tall pines pose in a fashion show,
Branches swaying to and fro.
A woodpecker drums a silly tune,
Avocado-green, beneath the moon.

In their shade, the foxes spin,
Designing hats with a cheeky grin.
Oh, what a wondrous sight to see,
Nature's jesters, wild and free!

Reflections in the Green

Mirrored leaves in puddles gleam,
Reflecting dreams that make us beam.
A raccoon twirls in snappy shoes,
While rabbits giggle at his moves.

The bushes rustle with gossip loud,
As passing clouds form a funny crowd.
With every twist, the green pokes fun,
In this dance beneath the sun.

Secrets in the Shade

Beneath the leafy green, they chat,
A squirrel plots with a chubby cat.
The pigeons gossip, so very loud,
While ants parade, so proud, so proud!

A raccoon juggles acorns with glee,
While bees hum tunes, as sweet as can be.
The shadows dance in a playful flick,
Nature's secrets, a fun little trick!

The Harmony of Nature's Breath

In the breeze, a frog croaks a song,
While turtles join in, though they're slow and strong.
A parrot squawks, throwing shade with flair,
As the trees sway and wiggle without a care.

The wind whispers jokes, swirling leaves high,
While bumblebees buzz, passing by with a sigh.
Nature's choir sings, a cacophony bright,
Turning dull moments into sheer delight!

Treetop Tributes

An owl in glasses reads the news,
While chipmunks act in their tiny shoes.
The branches sway in a pun-loving cheer,
Announcing the squirrel's career of the year!

The crows plot their heist of that lost bread,
While waking the slumbering bear's sleepy head.
The trees stand tall, with limbs open wide,
As nature's humor and fun can't hide!

A Tale Woven in Wood

Once a twig looked up, felt quite spry,
And dreamed of being a bird in the sky.
A scout squirrel teased, 'You wobble too much!'
But the twig just laughed, 'You're not all that such!'

Through sunlight's giggles and rain's soft sighs,
A tale unfolds among roots and skies.
With every chuckle, the forest grows bold,
As laughter among trees never gets old!

Treetop Tales: The Untold Rhymes

In a tree with a hat, sat a squirrel named Lou,
He sang silly songs that he thought were quite new.
But the birds laughed so hard, they fell from their perch,
And a raccoon joined in, with a comical lurch.

With nuts as his mic, Lou began to perform,
His dance was a sight, as he twisted and swarmed.
All the branches shook, with giggles and cheer,
Nature's own circus, a show every year.

Crescendo of the Wild

A bear tried to sing, 'Twinkle, Twinkle, Little Star',
But his deep voice shook the ground, and broke a few jars.
Deer stomped their hooves, in delighted surprise,
While nearby a raccoon was rolling his eyes.

The turtles were tapping, the frogs croaked along,
As the tree trunks echoed with this furry throng.
Who knew that a bear could carry a tune?
He swayed under branches, like a big furry moon.

The Language of Leaves

Leaves whispered secrets in a soft, breezy chat,
A chipmunk tuned in, wearing his grandpa's hat.
He nodded so wisely, you'd think he was sage,
While a spider spun webs for his grand family stage.

"Oh, tell me more tales!" the little ones squealed,
As the leaves rustled softly, their stories revealed.
Nature's gossip was sweet, with twists and with turns,
Filling up hearts with the wisdom they yearn.

Nature's Notebook: A Gentle Rhapsody

The sunflowers giggled as they tossed their bright heads,
And the tulips chimed in with their colorful threads.
A rabbit with glasses scribbled down notes,
While the daisies conspired from their leafy boats.

A fox in a bowtie came waltzing by slow,
He twirled in the grass, putting on quite a show.
Oh, nature's our stage, with laughs all around,
Where every wild critter can dance and astound.

Whispers of Leaf and Sky

In the breeze, a leaf takes flight,
Whirling 'round without a fright.
"Catch me if you can!" it cheers,
Rustling secrets, tickling ears.

Branches giggle with each sway,
As the sun smiles down all day.
Squirrels join in the playful chase,
Chasing shadows, they quicken the pace.

Symphony of the Sylvan Heart

Bugs and critters form a band,
Playing tunes of leaf and sand.
A toad hops in with a thump,
While a worm performs a jump!

The trees tap roots in a beat,
As the ants shuffle their tiny feet.
Rabbits join in with a dance,
In this forest, all take a chance.

The Dance of Branches in the Breeze

Branches twist like dancers grand,
Swinging low, they wave their hands.
The wind joins in with a laugh,
Spinning leaves, a playful gaffe!

Caterpillars do a spin,
Wiggling tails, they join in.
Bugs hold on for dear life's sake,
While trees quiver in the wake.

Reverie Among the Roots

Beneath the soil, a party brews,
With gophers wearing shiny shoes.
Rabbits toast with the finest clover,
Laughing as they roll right over.

Moles groove beneath like a wormy diva,
While a snail plays on its sweet old fifer.
In this world under the ground,
Laughter and fun are always found.

Verse of the Verdant Veil

In the garden, gnomes conspire,
Telling jokes around the fire.
A squirrel bakes a nutty pie,
While dancing branches laugh and sigh.

Leaves drop down with such delight,
Tickling bees that take to flight.
A mushroom wears a tiny hat,
And says, 'I'm really quite the spaat!'

Cadence of the Canopy

Beneath the shade of leafy dreams,
A raccoon knits with tangled seams.
It makes a scarf for winter's chill,
But ends up tangled; what a thrill!

The birds all chirp in silly tunes,
As squirrels dance to disco runes.
The owls wear glasses, oh so grand,
With wisdom odd, they misunderstand!

The Fable of the Forest Floor

A snail sells maps to wandering critters,
While ants discuss their secretitters.
A hedgehog juggles acorns with flair,
'Look at me!'—it's quite a scare!

The moss performs a wobbly jig,
While mushrooms join in, looking big.
It's a party on the soft, green ground,
Where laughter sprouts and joy abounds!

Dialogue of the Deep Woods

The trees exchange their sassy roasts,
About the fox who thinks he's boast.
A badger laughs, 'You call that style?'
While shadows shimmy, all the while.

A brook gurgles its witty talk,
As rabbits hop and mischievous stalk.
'You think you're smart?' a raccoon cries,
While all around, the humor flies!

The Story the Saplings Spin

In a grove where whispers play,
Saplings giggle all day long,
They tell tales of squirrels and hay,
In harmony, they hum their song.

With branches bent, they sway and dance,
A wobbly waltz, they spin around,
They dream of nuts and a romancing chance,
In the leafy theater, laughter's found.

The Chorus of the Chosen

Beneath the shade, a choir grows,
With trunks adorned, they belt out cheer,
Their barky voices, how it flows,
    Singing tunes for all to hear.

With roots like feet, they stomp with pride,
A rhythm made by nature's crew,
They joke about the bugs that hide,
In the branches where the breeze blows through.

The Rooted Reverie

In the soil, a party starts,
With sprouting shoots and tiny sprouts,
They parade with merry hearts,
Sharing laughs and joking shouts.

With worms as friends, they join in glee,
A rootball rave, a festive sight,
They spin and twist like roots set free,
In the glow of the warm moonlight.

A Crescendo of Canopy Colors

Leaves flutter down like confetti rain,
As branches wear their autumn best,
With colors bright, they entertain,
Joking about a leaf's great quest.

They gossip 'bout the changing hues,
With every rustle, laughter flows,
Challenging each other to choose,
Which shade will win the leafy shows.

The Heartbeat of the Wilderness

Squirrels dance like they own the place,
Tails a-twirling, keeping up the pace.
Rabbits hop with a fancy flair,
While raccoons rummage without a care.

A bear takes a selfie, posing just right,
Winking at the camera, oh what a sight!
Birds chirp gossip from high in the trees,
While ants march in lines, like they own the breeze.

A frog croaks loudly, calling for cheer,
"Join the wild party, there's nothing to fear!"
Nature's a stand-up, a real fun show,
Where laughter grows tall, and jokes freely flow.

Sketches in the Shade

Under the boughs where shadows play,
A chipmunk sketches in the clay.
With a tiny pencil and a leaf for a pad,
He draws all the funny things he's had.

A turtle looks on, quite impressed indeed,
Saying, "This art's slow like my speed!"
But the sketches take flight, they dance in the air,
As butterflies giggle, without a care.

A squirrel throws acorns – "Masterpiece!"
While a crow caws loudly, "Let's have some peace!"
Yet the laughter erupts, from the roots to the sky,
Nature's a canvas, so let out a sigh.

Whispers Woven in Wood

Trees whisper secrets, so silly they seem,
"Oak just fell over, lost his own beam!"
Maple laughs softly, despite the loud clatter,
"Don't worry, my friend, we'll just patch that matter."

Pine needles chuckle, tickling the breeze,
While vines tell tall tales with the greatest of ease.
Bark creaks with laughter, a voice made of knots,
"Knock, knock! Who's there?" – "Oh, leaf me some thoughts!"

Together they joke, a towering crew,
Making puns 'til the sun bids adieu.
In this forest of humor, all burdens take flight,
As laughter all day turns the darkness to light.

Trills of the Tall Trees

In the lofty branches where melodies dwell,
Birds chirp out tunes, ringing a bell.
"Why did the crow sit on the telephone wire?"
"Because he wanted to call, and the vibes took him higher!"

Owls wear thick glasses, looking quite wise,
But they misread the jokes, oh what a surprise!
"Why do trees never get lost at dawn?"
"Because they have roots, they can't go wrong!"

The wind joins in with a tickle and tease,
As leaves start to rustle in playful unease.
Together they sing, from branch tip to ground,
In the concert of laughter, joy is abound.

Symphony of the Leaves

In the wind, leaves rustle and jig,
A dance of whispers, quite the gig.
Squirrels conduct with frantic flair,
As acorns fall, flying through air.

Branches wave like jazz hands bright,
Imagine trees in a sheer delight.
Caterpillars groove on their way,
While mushrooms plan the next big play.

The sun plays trumpet, bold and loud,
Bees join in, making quite the crowd.
A symphony of branches and calls,
Nature's odd circus, where laughter falls.

So sway along, let your worries cease,
Join the leaves in a comic peace.
With nature's humor, we are as one,
In this silly concert, just for fun.

Dance of the Timber

The trees are boogieing, can't you see?
With roots that wiggle, they're quite the spree.
Watch the bark break into a grin,
As the trunks shimmy, let the fun begin.

Fungi spin like a top on the ground,
In the forest disco, joy is found.
Branches reach high for a sky-high twirl,
While pine needles flutter and whirl.

The forest floor hosts a funky beat,
With critters tapping tiny feet.
When the moon rises, it's party time,
Even the owls hoot in perfect rhyme.

So grab a partner, join the tree flings,
In the forest, all life sings.
With laughter echoing beneath the leaves,
It's the grandest ball, where nature weaves.

Resonance of Roots

Roots below are having a chat,
Discussing weather and the latest sprat.
"Who moved my stone?" one whispers low,
While another crackles, "It's just for show!"

They tickle the earth with tales from the ground,
Biographies of bugs that they've found.
With laughter echoing through the clay,
They agree, life's a rooty ballet.

The worms in tuxedos join with delight,
In this underground gala, what a sight!
While moles tap dance in their own style,
Making all who see stop and smile.

So beneath the leaves, let's celebrate,
Roots with their stories that oscillate.
In this hidden realm of giggles and cheer,
Every whisper and chuckle's crystal clear.

Secrets of the Sylvan

In the woods, secrets giggle and sway,
The owls whisper jokes from dusk till day.
Trees snicker softly as squirrels pass by,
In this shady realm, oh my, oh my!

Frogs in tuxedos croak a tune,
While fireflies dance under the moon.
Bamboo sways, it's quite the tease,
As rabbits hop 'round with the utmost ease.

Mushrooms gossip about the ground show,
While shadows play tag, two steps to and fro.
The breeze carries laughter, it's clear as can be,
These sylvan secrets, just wait and see.

So take a stroll through this enchanting spree,
Where nothing's quite as it seems to be.
With every leaf that rustles and sways,
Nature's laughter brightens our days.

Mossy Harmonies at Dusk

In the woods where moss does cling,
A frog jumps high, he's trying to sing.
The squirrels giggle, they can't quite hear,
As crickets chirp, full of cheer.

With shadows long and whispers sly,
A hedgehog sneezes, oh my, oh my!
A lost acorn rolls down the hill,
The giggly whispers are hard to kill.

The trees sway gently, branches prance,
As owls hoot loud, they join the dance.
Yet twilight chuckles, with its soft glow,
As all woodland critters steal the show.

So here we laugh in shadows cast,
With nature's quirks that never last.
The night falls in, we end our spree,
In mossy harmonies, absurd and free.

The Chorus of the Canopy

High above, where branches meet,
A wily raccoon taps his feet.
The leaves join in with a rustling sound,
While a bird drops a twig to the ground.

A bee buzzes in, quite out of tune,
While ants march forth as if in a swoon.
Their tiny feet create a beat,
In the chorus so silly, it's hard to keep.

With laughter shared and echoes bright,
The owls join in, what a silly sight!
They hoot so loud, bringing forth grins,
As the sun dips down, let the laughter begin!

The canopy sways to this jolly song,
All creatures gather; they can't be wrong.
In a world of fun, where laughter flows,
The chorus of the canopy always grows.

Radiant Reverence for the Green

In the garden where daffodils play,
A snail moves slow, savoring the day.
The sunflowers sway, they cheer him on,
As worms in the dirt prepare for dawn.

With every ray that brightens the scene,
A butterfly flutters, all shiny and keen.
It trips on petals, what a silly fall!
But up it gets with a floral call.

The veggies giggle, they're quite a sight,
As carrots poke out, oh what delight!
The radish blushes under leafy sleeves,
In the radiant revelry, everyone believes.

Here in the green, we laugh and reflect,
Nature's comedy, we can't neglect.
With joy in our hearts and sunshine so keen,
We celebrate all, in the joyous green.

Swaying Silhouettes at Twilight

As twilight whispers in soft lullabies,
Shadows dance funny beneath the skies.
A deer prances, tripping over roots,
While fireflies flash their little suits.

The raccoons wiggle, eyes all aglow,
Playing hide and seek, oh what a show!
The bunnies hop, with great big grins,
In a world where silliness always wins.

Branches creak gently, in the night's embrace,
As owls perch, looking wise at the pace.
Yet in the hush, a crackle, a snap,
As a mouse makes mischief within the trap.

So in the twilight, with laughter abound,
All creatures cavort, in shadows profound.
Swaying silhouettes share tales all night,
Crafting a world where all feels just right.

Hymn of the High Canopy

Leaves chat and gossip, so spry,
Squirrels dance under the sky.
Branches sway in a rhythm nice,
While a woodpecker's loud advice.

Breeze whispers secrets, trees chuckle,
In sunshine's embrace, they snuggle.
A chubby raccoon scurries past,
With snacks to share, just having a blast.

Dancing shadows perform a show,
Barking dogs with tails a-flow.
Nature's laughter fills the air,
A leafy party, beyond compare.

Fungi wear hats, proud and stout,
With glee, they shout, "Join our rout!"
Under the canopy's silly sway,
Life's a jest on this leafy stage.

Sonnet of Sunlit Glades

In dappled light, the branches beam,
While butterflies plan their bold scheme.
Grass tickles toes, laughter erupts,
As mischievous bugs give playful jumps.

A frog croaks jokes, a witty bard,
His audience, a deer and a yard.
With flowers adorned, somewhat wild,
In this glade, we're all nature's child.

Twigs snap underfoot—oh my, oh dear!
A raccoon laughs, "Watch where you steer!"
In sunlit patches, we roam about,
With giggles, nature's silly clout.

Peering through leaves, a secret delight,
Where squirrels vie for acorn's height.
Each shadow tells a funny tale,
In shimmering glades, we shall prevail.

The Call of the Canopy

Branches beckon, come take a look,
Find the stories in every nook.
Birds jest and joke, a feathery crew,
Swinging from limbs, they holler—"Woohoo!"

Lizards boast of their sunny tan,
While ants march, all in a plan.
The tallest tree spins tales of yore,
With laughter that echoes forevermore.

Breezes tease the leaves to sway,
While gopher pops up to play.
With acorns and giggles in tow,
Nature's pranksters put on a show.

As shadows grow long in jokes galore,
The laughter of trees is hard to ignore.
In this call of a whimsical spree,
The canopy sings, "Come laugh with me!"

Melody of Moss and Mirth

Moss carpets the forest floor green,
Tickling toes, a soft sheen.
Frogs croon ballads, ribbits in tune,
While leaves nod gently in the afternoon.

Squirrels trade snacks in a bartering spree,
"Your nut for my berry, oh, what a fee!"
Dancing mushrooms in playful rows,
Invite all the critters to join in their shows.

A shadowy cat makes a pounce,
Only to tumble, oh what a flounce!
Nature chuckles at every flop,
As giggles from bushes start to pop.

The melody of joy wafts all around,
In this woodland, pure laughter is found.
With every rustle, a chuckle is born,
In moss and mirth, we forever adorn.

The Tones of Tranquil Trees

In the forest of whispers, trees giggle tight,
With leaves as their voices, a joyous delight.
Branches dance sideways, a jig on the breeze,
While squirrels debate, 'What's better, nuts or cheese?'

Bark is the gossip, it scratches the air,
'Have you heard the one about the fruit that's bare?'
Their laughter erupts, as the shadows play,
Under the sunlight, they frolic all day.

The birds start their chorus, a cacophony loud,
While crickets join in, forming a proud crowd.
A chipmunk, quite chubby, leads all in a dance,
As the sun sets gently, they relish the chance.

With roots intertwined, they root for each other,
These trees are a family, each sister and brother.
Holding a concert, they flourish and sway,
In a hilarious orchestra, they'll always play.

Composition of Canopy Chronicles

Beneath the green canopy, tales intertwine,
Where the branches pluck stories, like grapes from the vine.
A woodpecker knocks, metronome on a spree,
'Is this a symphony or just a loud bee?'

Frogs croak like tenors, they strike a fine note,
While the leaves clap their hands, in a laborious quote.
An acorn dreams big, of regality bright,
'One day I'll be mighty!' it hoots in delight.

The wind carries tunes from the trunk to the crown,
A merry confusion turns laughter around.
The sun joins the party, with a gleeful wink,
Painting leaves golden, as trees rise and sync.

As night drapes its blanket, the stars join the fun,
The owls hoot in rhythm, till their battles are won.
The trees hold their secrets, their shadows the key,
In their leafy domain, there's joy beyond spree.

The Solace in the Silent Grove

In a grove where the laughter seems ever so near,
The branches confide, their messages clear.
A wise old oak chuckles, 'Listen to me,
Life's better in shades, with a cool cup of tea!'

The flowers gossip about fashion and trends,
'Who wore the best bloom? Grace or the bends?'
Daisies unite, spinning tales oh so grand,
While the breeze twirls around, lending a hand.

A toad stoops to ponder, a hat on its head,
'What's in for frogs? Or should I just tread?'
With laughter erupting like bubbles in stew,
The grove swells with joy, as the night wanders through.

Nature's ensemble, the critters take flight,
With twinkling-eyed fireflies marking the night.
In harmony's dance, where fun finds its place,
The silent grove hums with a whimsical grace.

The Graceful Gaze of the Treetops

Up high the branches laugh and sway,
Tickling clouds in a cheeky play.
Squirrels dance in a dizzy spin,
While birds chirp songs with a cheeky grin.

Leaves gossip softly in breezy tones,
Whispering secrets in dulcet zones.
A woodpecker knocks like a raucous friend,
Echoing laughter that never ends.

Sunbeams sneak through each leafy frame,
Painting shadows that play silly games.
As branches wave like a festive crowd,
Nature chuckles, vibrant and loud.

The wind twirls leaves with a playful shout,
"Catch me if you can!" it teases about.
With every twist, the treetops cheer,
As Earth spins on, never in fear.

Nature's Note: A Chorus of Color

Petals pirouette in a garden ballet,
Wiggling their hues in the sun's bright ray.
Bees belt tunes in a buzzing delight,
While butterflies twirl in a whimsical flight.

Dandelions puff as they take to the sky,
Imagine a wish with a dash and a sigh.
A raindrop giggles on a leaf's round crest,
Nature's rhapsody, simply the best.

The sun-flower beams, with a grin so wide,
"Come dance with me!" it calls with pride.
With grasshoppers leaping like stars in a spree,
The show rolls on, whimsical and free.

Each bloom and buzz plays its perfect role,
Creating a scene that tickles the soul.
Where the hues collide in jovial cheer,
Nature's note sings, sweet and clear.

Interlude of the Intangible

In shadows' cloak, the whispers reside,
A playful banter that can't be denied.
Goblins of mischief dance through the dusk,
Chasing the laughter that twirls with a musk.

Moonlight giggles from the velvet sky,
As fireflies waltz like sparks passing by.
Every rustle's a joke from the night,
Turning the silence into pure delight.

The trees wear shades of an evening gown,
While crickets chirp their jazzy renown.
A shadow does a jig between the lines,
Making mischief where the starlight shines.

It's a playhouse of whispers, never quite still,
With an audience of night, in joyful thrill.
Where every gust carries giggles anew,
A dreamy interlude, just meant for you.

The Saga of Shadows

Under the moon, shadows grow bold,
Wanderers tremble at stories retold.
Trees stretch arms to embrace the night,
While shadows plot mischief, just out of sight.

Odd-shaped phantoms do curtsy and bow,
Checkered and silly, they dance like a cow.
In the flicker of light, they prance and glide,
Mischievous tales that nature can't hide.

The owl's wise hoot is more of a jest,
A feathered comedian taking a rest.
Chasing away fears with humor so sly,
As twinkling stars wink and giggle nearby.

Under the cover of whimsical hues,
Shadows perform with their slapstick cues.
In the tapestry woven by night and by day,
Nature's mischief, forever at play.

Serenade of the Seedlings

In the garden, seeds do dance,
Swaying leaves, a green romance.
Worms waltz by in top hats grand,
While bees perform, a buzzing band.

Sunbeams shine with a golden glow,
Tickling petals, oh what a show!
A ladybug, with spots so bright,
Can't help but join the silly night.

Frogs play leapfrog, with hearty croaks,
Telling jokes as the breeze pokes.
Trees chuckle in their leafy coats,
Among the sprouts, laughter floats.

So gather 'round for this silly spree,
Nature's joy spills wild and free.
With every rustle, a giggle grows,
In this merry patch, anything goes!

Gentle Murmurs of the Grove

In the grove where whispers play,
Trees gossip in a jovial way.
A squirrel zips, a jester in flight,
Telling tales of his grandest bite.

The flowers blush, dressed in their hues,
Sharing secrets with the morning dews.
A chipmunk chimes in, oh what a sight,
Cracking jokes 'til late at night.

Shadows dance in the silver moon,
Grass sings softly, a merry tune.
Crickets laugh with their chirpy sound,
While the whole grove twirls round and round.

Oh what magic in this place so bright,
Where even the roots seem to take flight.
Join the laughter, let worries cease,
In this grove of whimsical peace!

Nature's Musical Embrace

Oh, listen close to nature's beat,
Where every leaf finds its own seat.
The wind whistling through branches high,
Is nature's laughter, oh my, oh my!

A raccoon strums on a bark-made drum,
While frogs croak like a jazzy hum.
The daisies sway, a sweet ballet,
As squirrels pull pranks in a shifty way.

Fireflies blink, a shimmering show,
With tiny lamps in a magical glow.
They twirl and swirl in skies so vast,
In this concert, none are outclassed.

So come and join, let spirits lift,
Nature's jesters, a merry gift.
In this embrace, don't be forlorn,
For laughter in nature is always reborn!

Enchantment of the Evergreen

Among the evergreens so tall,
The trees gather for a lively ball.
With pine cone hats and bark-clad suits,
They tap their roots to nature's flutes.

A hedgehog spins, while shadows sway,
As branches crack jokes in a punny way.
The owls hoot with a mischievous tone,
While the whole forest calls it home.

Crickets join in with a playful click,
As fawns leap in with a little kick.
The twilight hums a friendly cheer,
In enchanted woods, fun's always near.

So let's unite in this frolicsome space,
Where laughter and joy leave no trace.
In the evergreen's heart, glee is found,
Nature's magic forever unbound!

Echoes of the Evergreen

In the forest, squirrels play,
Collecting nuts throughout the day.
Trees whisper secrets, leafy and green,
While rabbits hop, all quiet, unseen.

A pinecone drops, thud on the ground,
And owls hoot softly, all around.
The grassy carpet, soft and spry,
Giggles of breezes make branches sigh.

Bamboo shakes, a dance on its own,
Wiggly worms in the soil are grown.
Nature's riddle, wrapped in delight,
In this green theater, laughter ignites.

The wind strums leaves like strings on a lute,
As critters gather, a woodland pursuit.
They ponder the jokes of the wise old tree,
Who chuckles at life, eternally free.

The Sound of Stillness

In quiet groves, a stillness speaks,
With crickets croaking silly squeaks.
A breeze brings whispers from high above,
Trees sway in rhythm, like they're in love.

Mossy chairs for the insects' jest,
Ants hold contests – who can do best?
Jays joke around, in colors that pop,
While bumblebees buzz, they just can't stop.

A frog croaks loudly, claims he can sing,
But all the birds just laugh in a ring.
Leaves chuckle softly, rustling playfully,
Life's a comedy under the canopy.

In this theater where no one's shy,
The trees roll their eyes as clouds drift by.
Nature's humor, a joyous spree,
Echoes of laughter in every tree.

Lines from the Lush Land

Where daisies dance, and daisies chat,
A hedgehog sneezes, oh, imagine that!
Raccoons wear masks, oh what a show,
While trees stand tall, just waiting to grow.

The brook chuckles, as fish take a dive,
With each little splash, they feel so alive.
A bear tries to waltz on a slippery stone,
And ends with a plop—he's clearly outgrown.

The sun paints smiles on petals bright,
While shadows tease, in the fading light.
Whistling winds carry tales of delight,
In the lush land's laughter, from morning to night.

Every creature joins in the festive cheer,
As nature's comedy unfolds year by year.
With every giggle and playful chase,
Life finds a way to fill every space.

Carols of the Creaking Limbs

Beneath the boughs where laughter swells,
The branches creak with ancient tales.
A woodpecker drums, in upbeat style,
While chipmunks scurry, bringing their smiles.

Curvy vines twist in a jolly dance,
Wiggly worms get lost in a trance.
Leaves burst out laughing, a leafy cheer,
As squirrels munch acorns without fear.

The old oak groans like a playful grandpa,
Sharing stories of old, in a funny quirk, ah!
Breeze tickles branches, causing a fuss,
Nature's orchestra plays, no need to rush.

As starlight twinkles, the night takes flight,
The trees hum tunes, both merry and bright.
Under the moon, the woodland sings,
In the laughter of nature, joy never clings.

Secrets of the Swaying Spruce

In the forest tall, a secret stood,
Swaying branches, misunderstood.
A squirrel danced with much delight,
Wearing acorns as a hat, oh what a sight!

Whispers of wind, they chuckled loud,
As the spruce swayed, a dance so proud.
Bumblebees buzzing, in silly lines,
Accidentally bumping into twines.

The sap dripped down, it laughed and blew,
Telling stories of trees it knew.
And all the critters gave a cheer,
For the spruce that swayed, no doubt, my dear!

Under the moonlight, they play charades,
With shadows dancing in leafy glades.
Each branch a player in this show,
But the squirrel steals the spotlight—don't you know?

Notes from the Nectarous

Buzzing bees in a nectar sweet,
Gathering laughs with every beat.
Florals giggle, petals sway,
In a honey trap, they play all day.

The lilies whisper with a wink,
Sipping sunshine, oh how they think!
'What shall we wear?' a tulip quips,
"In polka dots or a gown of strips?"

A bumble's laugh—like music, bright,
Bouncing past daisies in pure delight.
With each stop, there's gossip and cheer,
As flowers bloom, more jokes appear.

The nectar flows like silly syrup,
Dancing humbugs hear the stirrup.
In this garden of giggles and glee,
Nature's notes sing, "Join us, and be free!"

Reverie of the Rustling

Leaves giggle in a breeze so light,
Whispers travel, oh what a sight!
A child hides, peeking with glee,
'The trees are chatting, come and see!'

Breezy banter, a rustling sound,
A squirrel's chatter spreads around.
The branches gossip without a care,
Painting secrets in the air.

Beneath the moon, shadows prance,
As trees hold court in a nightly dance.
Who said wood was always still?
They party hard on a whimsical thrill!

And all the owls laugh in delight,
"Who knew trees could throw a night?"
The rustle rises to a joyful spree,
In the heart of the forest, wild and free!

Harmony of Humble Trees

In modest groves where laughter grows,
Lively beings, a funny prose.
Saplings chatter with leaves so green,
"Did you see that?"—a surreal scene!

The gnarled oak tells tales so grand,
Of a wayward branch that couldn't stand.
It trips and tumbles with such flair,
Only to twirl in the evening air.

Sunlight filters with a playful gleam,
Basking in each tree's daydream.
Caterpillars wriggle with clumsy pride,
"Join us here, it's fun outside!"

So reside, rejoice in nature's tease,
Where trees unite with the soughing breeze.
In this humble concert of happy hearts,
The laughter echoes, as joy imparts.

Enchantment of the Oasis

In a land where palm trees sway,
A lizard winks in bright ballet.
Cacti wear hats, oh what a sight,
And camels dance in the moonlight.

A parrot tried to sing a tune,
But all it got was a cactus prong.
The oasis chuckles, cool and clear,
As frogs croak jokes that all can hear.

With each drop of water, laughter flows,
The sun, a jester, puts on shows.
Dunes giggle as winds burble by,
While rabbits hop, oh my, oh my!

So swing by this sandy delight,
Where mirth grows strong in the hot sunlight.
Dance with the palms, sway with the breeze,
In this oasis, joy is the key!

The Echo of Elysium

In a meadow where daisies play,
The butterflies flutter, come what may.
A rabbit sings, a squirrel grins,
As flowers blush, and laughter begins.

The sun is a joker, bright and round,
Tickling the grass, joy is all around.
A bee buzzes jokes while sipping nectar,
While ants march on, a tiny vectra.

Clouds drift by in a cotton parade,
Where the shadows sing and sunlight is laid.
Each echo bounces, a giggling sound,
In this lush garden of joy unbound.

As dusk creeps in, the crickets cheer,
With soft serenades for all to hear.
Under the moon, the fun won't cease,
In Elysium, laughter finds peace!

The Dialogue of Dawn and Dusk

At dawn, the roosters start to joke,
While the sun giggles, gives a poke.
The sky blushes with orange waves,
As sleepy stars are misbehaves.

Dusk rolls in, with a wink and a grin,
The fireflies dance, let the fun begin.
Clouds whisper tales of day's delight,
While owls hoot, "What a joyous night!"

The sun pours coffee, and the moon takes tea,
They trade their secrets, so silly and free.
The crickets chime in with their own beat,
As the world spins on, their melody sweet.

With every tick of time's grand clock,
The day and night play a silly mock.
In this dance, we'll join and laugh,
As shadows and light write a comic half!

Nature's Lyric: The Timber Tale

In the heart of the woods where splinters speak,
Trees swap tales, both funny and sleek.
A piney fellow cracks a barky pun,
While poplars sway and join the fun.

The squirrels chatter, in a nutty craze,
While woodpeckers play in a rhythmic daze.
Moss blushes green as laughter flows,
And each leafy listener giggles and glows.

The river chuckles with rippling glee,
As fish in frolic swim wild and free.
"Why did the log cross the creek?" they jest,
"To float on over and take a rest!"

In this grove of giggles and cheer,
Nature spins tales that all can hear.
So listen close to the wisdom and fun,
In this timber tale, laughter's never done!

A Symphonic Grove at Daybreak

In the morning light, trees sway,
Doing the cha-cha, in their own way.
Squirrels are jiving, birds in a show,
Even the old oak seems ready to go.

A tree trunk trumpet sounds a loud honk,
While branches dance, doing their flunk.
Rabbits hop high, on the grass, they prance,
It's a forest party — come join the dance!

The sun peeks in, with a big goofy grin,
Not a leaf is quiet, all are in.
Leaves clap their hands, what a silly sight,
As the day breaks free, with laughter and light.

Chords of the Whispering Woods

In the woods where whispers play,
Trees share secrets in a funny way.
A birch tells tales of night's wild ball,
While snickering pines try to recall.

Mossy carpets giggle, oh so bright,
As logs roll over, what a sight!
Tune in, dear owl, don't miss the news,
A critter choir sings all the blues.

The trumpet vine plays a wacky tune,
While beetles dance under the moon.
With every rustle, laughter grows loud,
It's a raucous band, drawing quite a crowd.

Whispers of the Wood

The wood has whispers, soft and sweet,
Where every branch has a funny beat.
Mice are gossiping, tails in a knot,
While ferns gossip too, like they are hot!

A hedgehog chuckles, with spines so neat,
As he juggles acorns, oh what a feat!
Geese waddle by, giving side-eyes,
They point at a frog in a silly disguise.

The trees lean closer, ears perked in glee,
As a chipmunk claims he's the king of the spree.
Every leaf laughs, waving in the breeze,
Celebrating the wood, with giggles and wheezes.

Echoes of the Canopy

The canopy echoes, filled with delight,
As branches tickle the blue sky bright.
Parrots squawk jokes, making a ruckus,
While ants march in step, they're quite the focus.

Frogs play drums on the logs so slick,
The rhythm is wacky, but oh so quick!
Bumblebees buzz, with a tune in their wing,
Nature's own orchestra, ready to sing.

Laughter cascades down from leaves in the top,
As squirrels swing by, they just won't stop.
In this lively grove, joy fills the air,
Echoes of fun, everywhere!

The Language of Leaves

A leaf said to a twig, "You need a new style!"
"But I'm feeling quite fresh, just look at my smile!"
"You need a bit of flair, just a leaf-twist or two,"
"Please don't bend my branches, it's hard to look cool!"

The acorns are laughing, they roll in the grass,
While the squirrels are debating, who steals which stash.
"I swear I had one right here, beneath this oak's shade,"
But it's gone, what a mystery! All kinds of charades!

Breezes pass messages, tickling each limb,
The pines sigh their tales, looking rather dim.
"What's that rustle? A secret? I'm dying to know!"
"Oh, just the wind gossiping! Go put on a show!"

The old tree reminisces, wrapped in its bark,
"Once I danced with the clouds, oh, what a bright spark!"
"Now I just sway gently, with a few knots and pains,"
But the forest all cheers, as he sways in his chains!

Fragments of Forest Fantasia

In the woods, a beetle promotes his new band,
Playing guitar with twigs, he dreams of the grand.
"We'll fill the air with buzz, our songs will unite!"
And all of the critters agree it sounds right.

But the owls, they hoot from their branches high up,
"Your rhythm's a flutter—what's happened to the 'thump?'"
"We're just vibing, old friend, don't rain on our jam!"
The owls roll their eyes, "Just don't wake up the Gram!"

The ferns start to shake, passing tales of old days,
"When the moon hosted dances in the winds' wild ways!"
And the fireflies flicker, winking bright in the dark,
"Let's light up the night, and leave our own mark!"

A fox in a hat struts, performing a dance,
"With my moves, little friends, I'll put you in a trance!"
But the raccoons just laugh, spilling snacks on the floor,
"The forest is alive, who needs a dance tour?"

Twilight Whispers in the Woodland

The twilight wraps the trees in a velvety hue,
As crickets strum tunes, two beetles waltz too.
"Careful now, my friend, you're stepping on my toes!"
"Oh come on, dear partner, just follow the flows!"

The owls are debating, who's the wisest tonight,
"It's clearly me! I can see in the night!"
"But you said that last week, and I found it absurd!"
"Old age brings perspective—oh, please don't say a word!"

The shadows start dancing, twirling around trees,
Whispers of mischief float lightly on the breeze.
"Did you hear that last giggle? It's certainly clear,"
"The whispers have voices, I swear they're right here!"

The moon chuckles softly, casting light on the scene,
While the mushrooms all giggle, feeling quite keen.
"The woodland is buzzing; let's keep it alive!"
"As long as we're swirling, we'll always survive!"

The Ballad of the Breezy Boughs

On a windy day, the branches convene,
With gossip and laughter, the scene's quite a dream.
"Who wore that fine bloom?" one leaf pointed out,
"That's the work of the sun, let's all give a shout!"

The trees shared a chuckle, their bark rough with age,
As the squirrels performed on their woodland stage.
"Look at my brave leap, I deserve a big cheer!"
But the audience gasped, "That fall was quite near!"

The breeze danced between them, swirling and free,
"Now gather 'round friends, and come listen to me!"
With a twirl and a whistle, the air filled with glee,
"In the world of the trees, we remain wild and free!"

As dusk painted skies, they sighed with delight,
"Tomorrow brings more; let's be ready to fight!"
For another grand tale, with laughter and song,
In the ballad of boughs, where all critters belong!

The Euphony of the Evergreens

Evergreens sway with a humorous tune,
Their branches dance, and they chuckle at noon.
A squirrel sneezes, it spins in surprise,
While a bird in a bowler hat glares from the skies.

Pines gossip loudly of the oak's fancy leaves,
Playing chess with the maples, oh what a tease!
The wind joins the fun with a tickle and whoosh,
Sending acorns to tumble in a raucous push.

Beneath their tall shadows, giggles abound,
As shadows stretch long and play on the ground.
A raccoon in a mask pretends to be sly,
While the porcupines snicker at passing butterflies.

Laughter rings out from the roots to the sky,
Whispers of secrets that flutter and fly.
The trees hold a party beneath stars so bright,
Seeking new friends 'til the morning light.

The Woodlands' Woven Words

In a wood where the critters weave tales of cheer,
A fox juggles berries, oh what a great sphere!
The owls hoot riddles with a wink and a nod,
While a bumblebee buzzes, saying, "I'm a god!"

The branches gossip with leaves all aflutter,
Whispering softly like voices of butter.
A rabbit hops in, with a joke up its sleeve,
About a ferret who dared to deceive.

Old trees claim wisdom that's funny yet wise,
About how the sunset caught fireflies by surprise.
Their roots form a circle, where laughter is bold,
As the creatures exchange the best stories retold.

Drifting through meadows, the humor is free,
Where every tall fern is as tall as a tree.
In this woodland concert, all creatures partake,
With giggles that dance, make the silence awake.

A Saga of Seasons

Springtime arrives with a chuckle and sprout,
As the daffodils giggle, they fill with a shout.
Bumblebees bounce through the bright blooming bows,
Teasing the tulips with delicate vows.

Then Summer bursts forth with a splash and a song,
While the hot sun says, "Come on, tag along!"
The grasshoppers leap, making music with ease,
Conducted by crickets in gentle light breeze.

Autumn rolls in with a jacket of gold,
While pumpkins all prance, looking bright and bold.
The trees drop their sweaters, they dance with delight,
As squirrels make confetti from acorns at night.

Winter's a jester, with snowflakes like laughs,
Covering branches in cozy white staffs.
As the frost twirls a tale in a chilly embrace,
The woods hold their breath, just waiting for grace.

Melodies of Memory in the Forest

In the heart of the forest, where memories sing,
A woodpecker dances, making caverns ring.
With laughter and echoes bouncing all around,
The trees clap their hands with a splendid sound.

Flashbacks of picnics with ants on the rise,
The bear making tea, what a surprise!
The sun filters through leaves with a giggle so bright,
As the shadows perform in a whimsical fight.

Each path tells a story, each step is a play,
With the laughter of foxes and owls in a fray.
The memories linger like a sweet melody,
Weaving through woodlands, so wild and so free.

So come join the frolic, bring laughter you find,
In this forest of memory, leave worries behind.
For nature's a concert, vibrant and true,
With tales that will tickle and brighten your view.

Cacophony of the Canopied Sky

The squirrels dance in cheerful chaos,
Chasing shadows, forming a ballet.
Chirps and tweets mix in loud cacophony,
While leaves giggle, swaying in play.

Raccoons wear masks, playing peek-a-boo,
Tree trunks tickle, brush aside the gloom.
Bouncing branches play the tambourine,
As nature croons, we await its tune.

The owls hoot in humorous debate,
While the wind weaves tales with a twist.
Each knot in the bark tells a joke,
Under the canopy's playful mist.

And as the sun sets, the giggles rise,
Nature's laughter fills the dusky sky.
With every rustle, there's a surprise,
A fun-filled symphony, oh my, oh my!

Roots that Reach for Stars

Roots stretch out like legs in a race,
Seeking stars with a hopeful grin.
They trip on rocks, fall all over the place,
In gravity's hold, they can't quite win.

The wise old tree whispers a secret,
"Dig deeper, my friends, it's worth a try!"
But the roots just laugh, "We're not here to fret,
We'll take our chances, reaching the sky!"

With every tug from the breeze at night,
They jiggle and wobble, oh what a sight!
It's a root jamboree, a boisterous fray,
"Let's dance with the stars!" they cheer and sway.

So if you look up when the moon is bright,
You may wonder why trees seem to giggle.
It's just the roots wiggling with delight,
Playing hopscotch with the stars, oh so little!

Sunlight's Serenade Among the Pines

In the forest where shadows peek,
Sunlight plays hide and seek.
Pines sway to a radiant tune,
Wearing crowns of laughter, a joyful monsoon.

Branches bend, doing the cha-cha,
While sunlight giggles, "Don't go too far!"
A spotlight shines on the forest floor,
As pine cones tumble, "We want more!"

Hopping hedgehogs join the parade,
Twirling tulips begin to invade.
Every beam of light sparks a grin,
As rabbits loop in a merry spin.

With each flicker, a chuckle emerges,
Sunlight's serenade endlessly surges.
Among the pines, joy does reside,
In this whimsical woodland ride.

The Art of Arboreal Dreams

In a world where branches are canvases bright,
Trees sketch with shadows in the soft twilight.
Dreaming in colors of green and gold,
Their artistic flair, a sight to behold.

Owl on the limb, critiques the scene,
"Mistakes are just features in nature's machine!"
Squirrels add splashes with acorn ideas,
While the butterflies flutter and hop in their cheers.

A painted sky serves as the backdrop,
As trunks twist and turn, they just won't stop.
Nature's gallery, alive with glee,
Cleverly crafted so wild and free.

So come to the forest, take in the charm,
Where laughter and art set the heart's alarm.
In this arboreal dreamland, we all twirl and gleam,
Creating our tales in nature's grand scheme.

Rhapsody in Renewed Green

In a leafy dance, the branches sway,
A squirrel's acrobatics steals the day.
With acorns as hats, they leap so spry,
Nature's little clowns, oh my oh my!

Down by the stream, the frogs sing along,
With ribbits and croaks, a symphonic throng.
They'll hop on the beat, a froggy parade,
In this verdant world, no gloom can invade.

Trees don their coats, all dapper and bright,
In shades of chartreuse, a hilarious sight.
With whispers of laughter in every breeze,
They chuckle as tickled, they bend their knees.

So join in the ruckus, let joy take its flight,
Under canopies dancing in warm, golden light.
A fest of the flora, with wit in the green,
In this rhapsody's heart, all's merry and keen!

Driftwood Dreams: A Forest's Lull

In the twilight glow, the branches yawn,
Whispering secrets from dusk till dawn.
A raccoon in pajamas eats pies made of bark,
While owls debate who'll play 'nighttime shark.'

Mushrooms on stilts, they wiggle and nod,
Their caps like top hats, so very odd.
A party of shadows, they boogie and sway,
In this dreamscape wood, where odd meets the play.

Breezes with quips swirl 'round like a game,
Chasing the beetles, who shrug off the fame.
The crickets compose, with no fear of clowns,
Their serenade echoes through twilight towns.

So nestle with laughter, let night be the guide,
Dream driftwood wonders in this nature's ride.
In lullabies woven with chuckles and cheer,
We celebrate mischief in forests so dear!

The Poetry of Petals and Bark

With petals all giggling and bark full of jokes,
The flowers conspire with whimsical folks.
Bees buzzing tunes that are silly yet sweet,
As the daisies tumble, they can't help but tweet.

A maple, with leaves of a dazzling hue,
Shares tales with a willow, who sways when it's blue.
They chuckle 'bout seasons, the sun and the rain,
Turning gray days into joy without strain.

'Yet here comes a poodle in glasses,' they chant,
While a snail runs a marathon—quite the gallant!
The lilacs all cackle, while roses turn red,
In their world of blooms, laughter's never dead.

So gather the petals, and hear life's sweet jest,
In this garden of giggles, we're surely the best.
For nature's the poet, in all its delight,
With every green sentence, it sparkles with light!

Soliloquy of the Shadows

In twilight's embrace, the shadows convene,
With jigs and with jests, they frolic unseen.
A gnome in the corner sips tea with a squirrel,
While dancing with moonbeams makes their tails twirl.

Each whisper of darkness holds stories to share,
Like trees talking wildly of who cut their hair.
The whispering pines plot the best kind of jest,
And all of the owls join in, fully dressed.

With footsteps so light, they prance through the night,
As mischief unfolds with delightful delight.
The leaves rustle gently, their laughter spreads wide,
In the realm of the shadows, where joy's always tied.

So linger with giggles, let moonlight be gay,
In this soliloquy where pranksters play.
With shadows a-shimmer and humor's embrace,
In night's hearty laughter, we find our true place!

www.ingramcontent.com/pod-product-compliance
Lightning Source LLC
Chambersburg PA
CBHW071827160426
43209CB00003B/225